BEAUTIFUL & BATTERED

Breaking Through The Chains

ORKIDEDATTER

CONTENTS

ORKIDEDATTER

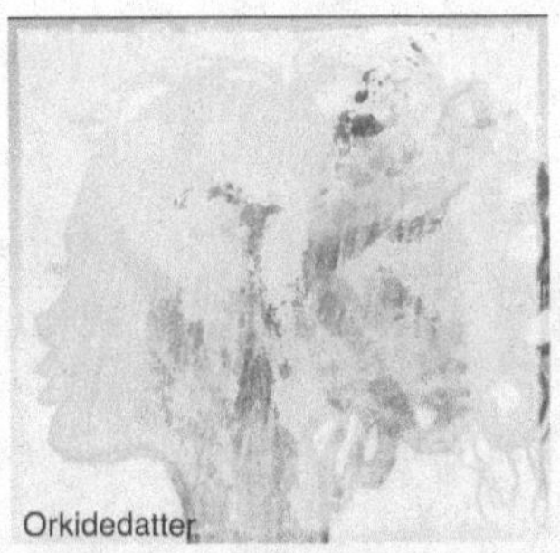

Orkidedatter

**From the north a butterfly in winter land
under the Polar star in the elongated small
country
-Norway-
If you listen carefully you can hear her wing
stroke rises from a descending black star
from a nightmare visions flash down below
the abyss.
Breaks through the chains from a cage of
another day healing subconsciously a picture
of pain.
Bleeding memories and a battered country
girl, but beautiful as the midnight sun.**

**Strong as the Northern Lights dances on the
black canvas of the sky.
She colors her soul`s landscape of a ruin to
an architectural masterpiece.**

Orkidedatter

PREFACE

Orkidedatter is an artistic poet, writer, and artist from Norway. From the time she was a child, she has drawn her feelings, stories, poems, or experiences. A childhood with experiences children should not have, she used this to process emotions. Orkidedatter was never recognized or accepted for having this ability. She buried and hid her talent far inside her soul.

For many years she wrote, drew, and painted and nobody knew about it. She dared not talk about this to anybody because she was bullied and worse things happened. Several thought it was fantasy, but in her hand, she stood with her life.

For many years, she kept her writings and herself as a writer hidden like a secret. Now she is on her way to find herself in this literary atmosphere. She has removed her secret chapter by chapter in her life the last four years.

At the age of 40, she realized she had to deal with her childhood and get help to deal with all her traumas. Orkidedatter found a way back to her artist's soul and writer's heart. Writing became a healing process for her and her poetry collection grew.

The book is based on her life and the poems are

written as twisted and dark as her experiences from a child's mind as she remembers it and from old notes and books she has kept. There is always a truth of hers in these poems, but the reader has to wonder what it is. She is also an artist and try to make a connection between what she writes and her art. She does this to emphasize her message, feeling, or action.

The poems are written without editing with a touch of sparkling brightness. She hopes that more people in the same situation will know that they are not alone and that there is a way out of the dark.

Dear reader:

Thank you so much for your choice of this book and support. It will take you on a journey to different places in your mind, heart, and soul.

You may come across a poem you feel is close to your heart. With my writings, I hope you feel a message of a human`s emotional register and a mind's landscape of hidden places that you maybe had forgotten. May your adventure come to life in your soul, take a minute to feel, welcome thoughts and dreams wherever it is dreadful or beautiful, then let it go.

This poetry collection is born because of me finally found my lost soul. In my writings, I found home.

I suddenly was standing on the edge, staring into the abyss where fighting, surviving, and being strong was only my choice.

This poetry collection is dark and touches several emotions we don`t often talk about. Still, it has a taste of love and brightness.

It was in my darkness I found my light…

It was in my darkness I fight for to a better version of myself…

It was in my darkness I got rid of what was not healthy for me, my soul, and heart.

Step by step, I built myself up again…

Easy, no, but it is worth it because, to get the opportunity to sense, feel and color my day in every color I know of is a gift.

A fragile white butterfly with broken wings finally found its color and learned to fly again.

Thank you so much.
Orkidedatter

WILD BIRDS FLY, TAME BIRDS IN CAGED DREAMS

Wild birds fly, tame birds in caged dreams
The scream of fear and a hideous hand
the devil`s demands around a grave
the moon shadow suffocates her last breath
a little girl`s silhouette fades away in the
    star dust
her skinny little body still has bones to be
    chained in
the age of nine
cold blooded goodbye she cried
but still chained to life
when the wild swans complained outside
even with their freedom
tame birds in caged dreams
a cage of gold but no golden days
black rose wreaths of sorrow outside
the devil and death fight inside her mind
a prayer from her naked skin
cold of shame
the devil roars at dusk and reflects in her soul
waiting to use her eyeballs as marbles
it is dark and the thin little body trembles
pain - solitude - hopelessness
a foreign howl in the abandoned area

they took everything
death owns her mind
knocking on her guilt
her poor heart who only knows the dark
is nameless the age of nine
dance of death
a disturbed lie of the angels chimes
the silence creeps into her spine
powerless she falls to the ground
no teddy bear to squeeze
death blew her last petal from the black
    rose off.

PROTECTION

She is not fond of change.
It's like her whole limit is turn down.
She looks bit by bit to the ground, and it
    hurts.
She lays down and close her eyes.
In her mind she spreads her black cape
    over her.
From above, she looks like a black rose.
Beautiful, shiny and with a touch of redness
in its outer leaves.
Rose petals for rose leaves encircle her body
and fit perfectly together.
Some call it self-care.
She calls it protection.
Protection against the world.
Protection against pain.
Protection from who she is.
Protection from where she has been.
Protection from where she is going.
A little break from life.
Just find the heartbeat.
Feel ...
Breathe ...
Thoughts ...

Protect ...
and get ready for a new day, a new challenge
    and a new mastery of life.
Every day is a struggle for life.
Every day she picks up broken pieces.
Every day she glues the broken pieces
    together.
One day she is a glued scar in the soul on her
    way to new
adventures.

BURNED

You fight me off like a firefighter
so tell me why I still get burned
you pull away and I come in closer
and all we ever stay is torn
it hurt and it hurt so bad
I am burned and I will not be anymore
since my love up and got lost on me
and every breath that I've been taken
is like a torn on a rose
it hurt it is hurt so bad
I miss the tone of your heartbeat
it is such a warming and familiar sound
I hope you're finding the power
it hurt and it hurt so bad
To help you make it through the
darker day
if you want to take my breath away
I been near an angel
when you and me came together
hell to heaven and you were my
escape
it hurts and it hurt so bad
fires don't burn forever
I can't take away your love

we are faded to dust and it is
all these ashes crumble when
we touch
it hurts it hurts so bad
you`re breaking my heart, and I am
falling apart
we danced to death in the fire
and one day we want to arise
it hurt it hurts so bad
when I got burned.

LOVE IN THE WILDERNESS

He put his strong arms around her,
and she melted in his arms.
She felt his love and energy burn
around in her body.
She felt safe as he surrounded her
in nature's own wilderness.
Only the two alone against the
dangers of darkness.
Only the two alone against the
longing for love.
Only the two alone against
forbidden love.
His eyes told her about
sorrow and pain.
Her eyes told him about unknown waters.
He makes her do things she thought
she should never do.
She becomes a slave to his lovemaking.
They cannot remove each other's heartbeat.
They throw away each other's time.
Hope they will be happy in others' arms
     one day.
They spend a lot of time on a battle
that is already lost.

They tear each other's world apart.
Their hearts bleed and their
souls have caught each other.
They have given each other's life to eternity.
-Because, their strength of love nobody
dare to disturb-

VALUABLE

Butterflies cannot see their wings.
They can't see how beautiful they are.
But everyone else can.
I'm also like that, and I think many with
    me are.
Only we humans could start to see ourselves
a little from above and outside ourselves.
Can you?
What do you see?
Imagine waving your wings a little.
In a glimpse of magic, you will feel how
unique and meaningful you are.
Hold on to this feeling.
Feel what you are experiencing in this.
At this moment.
Your beautiful heart.
Your beautiful soul.
You are valuable just the way you are.

GHOSTSOULS FROM THE NATURE

Nature's most beautiful souls have
been sawn and cut down.
Have been driven over, stepped on and
shuffled off by an excavator.
Many of the beautiful trees have been swept
    up by
the root and shaken up and down.
Something is gone, but a lot is left.
The trees are pushed together to smithereens
    and
back there are large, dark and gloomy piles.
Piles of beautiful trees and shrubs that have
faded with their splendor.
It's like a burial mound.
It feels like it is shouted by pain from the tree
    souls.
Some deer stand by the dark piles.
There were once green and succulent buds
that tasted of nature's purity.
The deer scramble in the mound.
Around the fragile deer legs, dust and mud
    splashes.
Dust that lies like a ghost over the beauty that
    once was.

No grace in this world.
Man against nature.
Can the beautiful tones from rippling autumn
    leaves
color the spring's raindrops again.
It is like the bones rustling from the inner
chamber of the dust.
Fragile the brave nature's own voice withering
    away.
They stick well.
I can glimpse ghost souls from nature who
    painfully
struggle for eternal life.
It becomes empty, left behind it is just a
    ghostly landscape
that can give the darkest dark goosebumps.

WHY YOU DARE

She feels shattered and broken.
She is tired of always having to adapt to
    others.
She loves to go her own way.
She is always looked strange at.
Been never included because she thinks dif-
    ferently.
She is not like everyone else.
She dares to say what she thinks.
She has been laughed at, mocked, bullied and
    beaten.
Her words are not worth anything.
Many have turned their backs on her.
She has some wonderful souls in her life who
always stay when others go.
When she now creates her own world
    they are
knocking on her door.
They ask to come in.
They ask to participate in what is happening.
They will be part of her life now.
She thinks back on all the bad memories.
She was standing outside looking at the
    happy

people laughing and playing together.
She thinks back on all the times she got
     negative
answer because she was ugly.
She thinks of all the times she got negative
     answer
because she just wastes for the others.
She thinks of all the times she got negative
     answer
because they said she was weird, stupid,
     fat and
had the wrong clothes.
She can remember the feeling every time the
     popular
girls tore out her heart and trampled and
     twisted it.
Each time she had to swallow hard and bite
     her tongue
to blood because she was called too weak
     when she cried.
In a life with a darkness that not many people
     know about,
she is filled with light and love after all.
She wants everyone welcome no matter who
     you are.
But she wonders why you dare to knock on
     her door?

THE SHADOWS ON
THE BARN

In the beautiful breeze of the sunset
the shadows mirror nature beauty is
in the color of love.
In one with nature and under the sign
of freedom she dreamed
that she was dancing.
She danced in step with the rush of the trees
and from her heartbeat.
The wind shook in her long light hair
and hers summer dress surrounded
her fragile body.
The shadows moved in interaction with her
mind and soul.
She put her toes in spring-feathered grasses
gently was wiped out by the silence of
    darkness
that lay down as a robe over nature's
    landscape.
The shadows danced their way into her
    emotional
eternity.

A BRUSH STROKE

For every time she picks up the brush and
    looks
at the colors in front of her, her heart
will sing a happy song.
When she decides what color she should
    wear on
her coat, her soul will rejoice.
As she lets brush and paint become one,
her feelings of pain scream, and one brush
    stroke
reminds her of what was.
She can have bright and happy colors, but
still a shadow is thrown over them.
She can choose sad and dark colors and yet a
shadow is thrown over them, so they become
    even darker.
She can use the brush quickly with specific
    coats.
Or use the brush gently with light
    movements.
For each brush stroke there is a feeling.
The more she paints, the more "she" appears
in the games of color. Her innermost is re-
    flected

in what is painted in front of her.
She shakes her breath trembling and holds up
what she paints in front of her. In a moment,
a glimpse of the ghosts and a little glimpse of
    pain,
she can see something changing.
She hangs up what she has painted on the
    wall.
Take a few steps back and with admiration in
the eye she sees the shadows getting
    smaller and
the colors became clearer.
Can she master to let go...
Can she color over what was with new
    colors...
Can darkness brighten again...
What colors will she paint on her fragile
    wings
that will learn to fly?
She wipes away some tears, tears falling
    from the
depths of her heart and covering her soul
    with ...

HER SPIRIT

She hears you screaming at night and your
Voice is filled with grief.
Her curtain fluttering and she can feel your
    breath.
She lifts her hand to her heart
and it feels like drums, and she can`t stand
    still.
Her spirit dances in the flames along with
demons and elves in the night sky she
    follows you
wherever you go.
She needs you and admires you.
Take her with you
She is yours.
You`re not dangerous
The "Dark Prince" comes closer with his
violent tongue.
You call her…
She continues to dance around in a ring.
The wind grabs her soul and heart.
Her spirit stops for a moment.
Need help from the goodness of light.
She protect for her freedom,
but she can`t resist beauty.

Your poisonous heart is like a
snake who wrapped around her
and she can`t breathe.
Please, put an end to her pain.
You laugh and throw off your shadow in the
    flames.
You grow larger and powerful.
She is lost.
Spirit, soul, mind, and heart,
believe and fight.
She is yours.
Live and die.

A SEED

As she saw the
shadows moving
slowly, so she felt her
heartbeat in her chest,
the moon's magic myth spread
around her, and she felt cold.
The shadows glanced around her heart,
the moonlight shining
on her face
writhing in pain,
and her soul fighting
for her justice to
life that was about
to end. Worn she lay
on the ground
and scratched.
Into eternity, she
was to win and
the seeds of
life were sown.

POISONOUS WORDS

When she talks to you,
you arouse her feelings.
When she talks to you,
you arouse her experiences.
When she talks to you, you arouse
her whole "life", she tries to heal.
It is like knives being carved
in her heart and barbed wire
that tightens into her heart.
The heart bleeds and her soul
is twisted in pain.
It hurts.
Their blood band is invisible,
but for her it always bound.
It hurts.
She takes a step back and
lets poisonous words pass by.
She welcomes they, and let it go.
It is like a cold winter's night
that icicles flies like arrowheads
thrown into her skin.
It burns, and the scars have a pain
she can't describe.
They begin to fade,

the heart of her heals,
and the soul is flourishing.
She turns her back to the
words of poison
and goes away, but
the feeling of being always
inept, guilt and shame
is like burned in to her spirit.

THE NORWEGIAN FORCE

A stream of emotions
rinsing through her body.
Where the blood bubbled
through her veins,
and she can feel the
Norwegian force take
her back in a bygone era.
At the top of the mountain
she stretches her arms out
and can feel all the lost souls
who try to find home.
The heart rhythm is like
a large drum that surrounds
the whole of nature's own beauty
with strong rhythms.
Her skin can sense the magic
power that rises up the hills
and stays in one with the sky.
She has a bonfire in her heart -like
sparkles of energy.
Her spirit feels the peace,
it dances in the
Northern Lights.

THE DARKNESS

She can feel the darkness creeping
up her body
knocking on her bones
her heart full of emptiness freezes
her mind speaks a
language she does not understand
she wants to feel passionate love
she has so much to give
She fights and does not want to
fade away
she is not ready to go
she escapes
the past will always catch up with her
her mysterious side
waiting to be discovered
alone with her mind
alone with her soul
in the dark alone
with her heart of scar
eternal contact with the darkness.

THE SECRET

He loves her when she
is a secret.
Her heart is swelling with
emotions.
She twists her tongue and
her blood is rushing.
She feels stars in his eyes.
Her lips shape his name.
He tastes her lust delightful.
Bodies lick with motions.
Her fingertips on his chest.
He grab her hair and napping
to her neck.
She is drowning in his arms.
He embraces himself around her.
She kisses his lips slowly.
He breathes harder.
She satisfies all his wants.
He smells her desire.
She can feel his heartbeat.
His fingers dance along her jaw.
Whispering something in
her ear.

No one else know.
Her flames of passion
as you plunge within her depths,
and write her into his story.

UP FROM THE ASHES

She gets up from the ashes.
She doesn't know if she's dead or alive.
The eyes feel like coal.
She cannot recognize her body.
She listens.
Feeling her heartbeat.
It is empty.
Feels heavy.
Is it dark?
What grief was she.
What pain did she get.
What love should she choose.
She goes beyond the landscape that shines.
She sees a river.
She lifted her eyes.
She sees green meadows around the river.
At the river under a tree stands a man.
She looks back and a sorrow fills her whole
    soul.
Behind her it is hot and flames are thrown
against her.
She glimpses the colors of orange, yellow and
red that flutter.
It hurts.

She has come to the end of life.
Which way should she choose.
She chooses to go against the man.
He stretches his hands toward her.
She hesitates for a moment.
Life is shown in review in her mind.
There is nothing to go back to.
She chooses a foreign door.
It opens.
She feels hope, faith and joy.
The scars must heal.
She is alive.

DIFFERENT

You are not like the others.
Her soul is drawn towards you
over mountains and sea
landscape and city.
The wind has turned.
Inexplicably she becomes different.
Heartbeat can find each other.
You are something else.
Pictures of you play a movie in her mind.
You color your world with new colors.
Outside the limits the vibration
can explore your spirit
and for every
breath that you've been
taking is holding on to liberty.
She is trapped.
She is trembling.
Her voice begins to break.
Her eyes are filled up with tears
falling down her cheek
they come from her soul.
Protects her mind.

A DESIRE

She crumbled like hot wood in his hands.
She placed one hand
carefully around his neck.
She can feel his breath.
She feels his chest went
up and down in
pace with his heartbeats.
She rested her lips close to him.
She senses his passion.
Longing to have her.
She hears he sighed her name.
She swallowed, and a lovely laugh with
love got out of her mouth.
An endless moment and she lost herself
in his arms.
She laid her head back and leaned carefully
into him.
He kissed her slowly over her neck
and her breasts.
His hands began to explore her body.
With a smile on her cute lips.
An explosion approaches.
He grabs her long hair and pulls it

Backward.
Looks deep into her sparkling eyes,
and she rip off his desire for her.

COLORING YOUR DAY

Much we will meet
we must master many things
get up and listen to the day
the sun`s rays
that arouse your feelings in you
white butterflies wing strokes
what color do you choose today
the path is as new as yesterday
a new chapter in your life
must be written
listen to the depths of yourself
feel your heartbeat
feel your pulse
the fjord is as blue and shiny
as it flows like blood in your veins
you glance catches me
feel the darkness when the day is over
there is more we can still feel
what we can understand
the moon is just as new
but is just as secret
as the day tomorrow
the distant hills of nature remind us
about a bygone era

will never return
with the next morning break you can
make your best day
you can hear someone whispering
you in the ear
that everything should be well done
not be afraid
as a white butterfly should be colored
so can you choose your color of the day
make it your best with great love.

TIRED HEART

He opens her eyes to another world
with a lot of mysteries muddling her
she is a little insecure
makes mistakes
lost control
but are not afraid of what could
go wrong
he completely captures her
make her believe again
her light within begin to shine
her tired heart survived a
tropical storm when her heart cried
he makes a movie in her mind
so pure
so soft
so perfect
she made it a part of her soul.

PARADISE

She feels her heart beats in
the dark of night
He is her light
She is pain
He is colorful
No one understands her soul as he does
Nobody can put her heart on fire as he does
Her pure skin he gently touches
her lips with
Kissing
She feels fear
He is fearless
He invited her into his paradise
She can't find the words
Just whisper his name
Heal her
Ease her pain
Embrace her with a circle of love.

NEVER LET ME GO

He has the most sensual touch
I've ever felt
he has an understanding that my
soul has longed for
his words give me tears in the fire
I'm like a blizzard
he tries to tame me
every bud of my goose skin
craving his skin which embraces me
I am his frozen rose
he makes me melt
to a river flowing through
all of him
your heart
feels my heartbeat
my body has a desire to be twisted
in his body
hold me tight
never let me go.

MY STAR

I could have stopped the world for you
you've given me something to lose
the world can hurt me
I can't fall in love
broken is the silence
from my soul that
writhing in pain
the demon leaves my wounds
leaves deep scars
my heart is raining inside
on the outside the tears fall
Can not stop
it hurts so much
puts me down
chlorine in the ground
no grace in this life
will not die
will not live
it hurts every gang
we say goodbye
I'm making your dinner
to mine in my soul
of a ghost

i my darkness
there you are my star.

MY DEMON

She wakes up when you are knocking
on her bones
with your claws
you crawl over her like
the night of darkness embraces the moon
she can feel your skin
warm and soft
from the moonlight smiling in
she glances at your movements
with your feathery wings you`re
stroking her body
are you a demon or an angel
she gets goose bumps and shakes
when you put your legs around
her hips
you knock on her coffin
of a dripping rose bud
she understands that you have the key
your tool feels heavy where it is
pounding against her soft pillow
her body twists of desire
you grab her hair
scratches her cheek
she is labeled

she is yours
she can feel the smell
of your energy
she bites you gently
sucks and licking
you twist your tongue down her neck
she wants to kiss all the hidden zones as
is meant just for you and her tonight
as the stars shine and flash
the moon rises higher
you take her to a place
only you know about
this is your heaven.

THE BLACK ROSE

She is like a black rose
in the process of fading
he takes his lips
to each a petal
cut them off
it hurts
he lets them fall to the ground
they remain as
a shadow of her soul
he peels off her rose petals
finds her milky white skin
with the greatest tenderness
she never felt before
naked
an open book
colorless wings
endless shattered
her silence was a monster within
her darkness felt numb
she unfolds herself
with his strong arms around her
his sensual voice make
her crave for more
make her scream out loud

every bleeding scar in her heart
makes her tears of blood
take out the aching rose torn
and make her beautiful again
with the colors of the rainbow.

I`M FALLING LIKE A STAR

I'm falling like a star
he looks great in everything or nothing
he is the voice I love to hear
he is like a bubble bath and candles
he is like champagne and strawberries
he is like deep dark red roses
unresolved each petal
he is like a blizzard and silent ocean
I'm falling like a star
take fifteen minutes to kiss goodnight
I mesmerized all about him
he is the song I put on replay in my mind
he is the poem I not dare to write
I remember the first time I saw him
trying not to stare
he enchanted me when his eyes met mine
he is a good conversation
I wouldn't miss for nothing
I'm falling like a star
he is a picture in my wallet
he put all my ripped pages into my heart
    again
and kissed my scars to fade
he makes me feel alive and colorful

he fits perfectly within my soul
he melted her frozen heart
he is all the things that I long to and have
faith to and always misses
I'm falling like a star
let us catch each other's heartbeat and
wrap ourselves in the dangerous spider
web of love
will you survive by making love on my
polar bear fur in front of the fireplace
in the spooky midnight hour...

TORMENTED BY THE GHOSTS

In my bloodshot eyes I keep
staring at the moon
emptiness
hollow
sorrowful
I turn back time and remember
our bodies entangled together
in the darkest nights
I'm tormented by the ghosts
of the many souls who
touched my heart
all their words is laying like
a dusty fog all over me
I try to fight but the remnants
of war is tearing me apart
I`m still feeding my melodies of
you with poisonous liquid
elixir of magic
I hope it will kill my vibes for you
until then I take my demons with
me and disappear into the
shadows of the forest before
I paint the green leafs red...

A LITTLE PIECE OF HEAVEN

In the sunset breeze with the hearts on fire
every time he looked at her
with his diamond eyes
she was ready to sink
into the ocean of tenderness.

A little piece of heaven
don`t let the memory fade
the nighttime disappears like
last drops of an Angels tears
where did her broken heart go.

Is this the last dance to set
the world on fire with a spark within
the burning earth was made for he and her
she is lost but not forgotten
her ghost and spirit is hunting your soul.

She rip the wall down for you
you can`t hide from her melodic path
she ran through all your veins
why are you tearing her apart
is this her summertime sadness.

From your sharp heart you are cutting
        into her
she is the crying dove
not strong enough like a jewel
while falling in love and finding solace
in your sanctuary she is soaring.

Her frozen black rose petal falling
down to the ground she hopes not
she will open her wounds again
under the sapphire moonlight
he was the elixir to rise higher
She could feel the pain in her
crushed bones and her shattered dreams
her spirit floated on a cloud among the
        darkest night sky.
Not a single star was bright
a soulless girl in endless darkened back alley.

A QUIET PLACE

A quiet place
can feel the silence
tears from wrong side of heaven
a dark dilapidated bridge
abyss below
the last word are never said
the last cruel laugh is never ending
the last drop of blood are never spilled
the evil eyes are always awake watching
the poisonous tongue are always waiting
licking lips
longing for her milky white skin on her neck
a desire to bite her body until she screams
then the quiet place is not silence anymore
always remain in inferno.

MONSTER LOVE

She is in love with a monster
darkness a dark as her shadowy secrets
you are longing to find the key
silence like a lioness hunting
silence like a butterfly sparkling in the
frozen water
now is your moment to break her down
heavy like raindrops from her battle
yesterday that dried like the tears on her
cheek in her desolation
are you lingering in her shattered heart
she can't breathe
with your silence you are killing
her softly
your feelings fade
her memories don't...

BACK FROM THE EDGE

In every window I`m looking through
I see you...
you are screwing with my mind
you crushed me into pieces
I'm bursting into flames of your curse
I'm floating around in your doomsday
among with you all broken hearts from
beautiful girls
I've been doing things I shouldn't do
complicated
looking for love in a stranger's bed
a secret
back from the edge
my friends go crazy
I will always be your prisoner
my demons will always dance
with your control
pain burning like hell
when I heal
I come back with my own story
to tell
and this girl reach for the stars
and you are in my eternity of the
lost souls...

END OF THE LINE

She looked into the mirror
3 little scars from once she tried to
cut her face off
want to be faceless
deep into the mirror
her soul of sorrow
a message
4 little words
you don't deserve it
have a desire to find her beauty
her eyes widen in wonder
all she saw were her crying
shadow dancing
tears that filled up her eyes
falling out like blood
burning for every drop
the drops of blood form a pattern
of ashes and smoke seeps
flash dance
she will endure
life is a battle
been through worse
she buckles down
feel so cold

no rewind
no solution
no victory
time does not heal all wounds
she must learn to live with the scars
pick herself off the floor
protect herself
create her own universe of the beasts
close her eyes
-end of the line-

HEAVEN FROM HELL

It's buried in my soul
shadows deep inside
into the dead of night
zombies like to hide
watching me fall
breaking down
blackout
do you catch me?
Frozen I hold my breath
I died a bit every day waiting for you
hoping you could take my pain away
I get insecure
I'm so ashamed
emptiness
disaster
heaven from hell
heroes for ghosts
I can feel the fire below
meal the devil
and all the liquid do the colors in
the flames
A new day is born and it hurts.

A HEART OF TEARS

She tries to find peace because her heart will
    grow.
It's beautiful, but worn.
The edges are sharp all the way around.
It has been attempted repaired.
With needle and thread or patch.
If you look closely, you can see the
shade of the patch torn off time and again.
Looking even further in, at the back of the
heart, you can glimpse a face.
It can become clearer the more you see, or
more like the shadows waving in the wind.
Unclear with black color that slides into
each other and it becomes difficult to put
into words
- who it is -
You realize that the face belongs to the
heart, because they are equally ghostly.
She turns her face away in disgust and
loathing.
It storms in the heart's rhythm.
Faster and faster, she will not be anymore,
but it will not go away.

It is like thorns from "the black rose" being
thrown at her, and she feels an
indescribable pain in her heart.
In the face behind the heart tears flow like
a waterfall.
As a veil, they lie around her heart and dig
"the river of tears" bigger and deeper.
Can she fix it?
Can she be whole again?
Is the last flame extinguished?

She feels her heart, breathes deep,
tries to find calm
and feel her own heart beating.
They said it would be good again…
I don't need to take care of memories that
      aren't
good for me anymore.
She wipes away the tears that quietly fall
down her cheek.
Her body remembers.
The heart knows.
Her mind can trick her.
All the emotions and experiences are
stuck in her body as the pain of a thorn
they scream the worst she senses.
Her body is crying for help, her soul is
working on a blow to heal, her mind is
trying to work with heart.
And her heart ... she tries the best she can
to put it back together, so she can move on
in life.
With a heart full of scars she begins to feel
the various nerves. They are there as black
paths. Trails she never wants to join, but
they must be in ok condition.

They'll be with her to the end of life and,
she'll try everything she can to make new
paths bright and beautiful
next to the dark ones...

THE FOX GIRL

A little girl trapped in a house
doors and windows opens and closes
without being set free
at night she escapes into the forest
under her favorite tree, she looks at the
stars in the sky
have a desire to be among the stars
her best friend becomes a fox
she felt blessed
mocked when she talks about it
being called the fox girl
all beautiful words she makes a picture of
.....that does not exist....
Every night she goes back to the forest
she is called the daughter of the forest
she seeks comfort in her friend
the fox is always present with its beautiful
red fur and wise eyes
the lock on the window is reminiscent
of a past when she lost her freedom
it wasn't safe out in the night and
darkness they told her
she has never felt safer
she missed her friend so much

....pain....
A Man came and talk big of his rifle
she was a little girl, but she understood
she wanted out
she wanted to fight for her friend
the fox meant everything to her
can't have such a beast of prey around the
house they said...
Two scared little crystal blue eyes saw them
from her window
talking and laughing
helpless
she heard the gunshot
....she fell to the ground....
Her spirit…her soul…her heart
that day she was allowed to go outside
she never forgets her best friend's eyes,
and the fox stiff cold lifeless body
that day....
The little girl died inside.

CAN`T LET GO OF BEAUTY OF DARKNESS

In the night of horror she
became a vampire
tells a story beyond
monsters within have slayed her hope
in her darkest moments these monsters
comes out and play
reminds her of darkness who pushes
her to the edge
- but she can't let go of beauty of darkness
a whispering voice deep inside
challenging her sanity
how fight the monsters under her skin
who scratch her so hard that the
blood oozes out like a river
in a glimpse of light who roam hers
shadow and frightening mythical
signs in her tears
she cracks like her broken heart
finally her soul is free from spirit
of the wood nymph and the beautiful
moonlight streaming down upon her.

SHADES OF COLORS

If I can show you my devilish dreams
it can be a perfect soundtrack
I can tell you everything and
you can forget it because it makes you
blush forever
you will rip of my clothes and I'm
standing there naked
and I'll let you spill your ink on
every shape of my body and use
your feathers to makes me yours
shades of colors, you can create me
perfect
you have a desire to tell me everything that
will make my mind go crazy and my heart
will rhythm to your heartbeat, but I
scared you with my quivering
skeletons hide in my closet
please, don't hold back the words
because you are afraid to be hurt
I will smack your walls down
with my naked body and you will
let love in
only my skin and bones twisted around
your toxic body and mind

embraced with a sensation of death
simply for loving
you don't have to be alone and cold
in your peaceful bed when I can
make it warm with my ignite of
the devil's shadow beyond your
imagination
loving me will leave a burning mark
in your soul...

THE BROKEN INSIDE ME

Precious memories on a straw where each
    and every
water pearl from autumn colorful leaves left
    on the
ground waiting for to be crushed.
They shine like a jewel of the hours of my
    life.
A jewel in my heart of her orchid garden.
My precious memories of you are somewhere
    in
the shade behind the sunset.
Reminiscent of spring`s longings under the
    sapphire moonbeams
before sunrise took the treasure Chest
    with its.
My veil is falling - a source of hope.
You are my tenderness, but a remoteness
    during
the rainbow`s lamentation.
You weave your magic around my heart and
    you have
bound your spirit into my soul
and your ghost in my tears continue to
    humble down.

One drop touch my wolf tattoo and it
    shakes me
to the broken inside me.
I never forget the tears you brought into my
    soul,
but I brought you waves,
and they are moving and slaying you slowly
    without you knowing it.
One day you are coughing dust and suffocate.
You turned off a star, so I stayed in the dark.
You turned off the moon, so I would get lost.
You turned off the sun, so I started to decay.
Like pearls on a string I tied a wreath of pre-
    cious memories and words,
but I will always have a life without pastel col-
    ors, a life alone.
I was his words that made him cry.
We made love between fencing swords, be-
    cause I was never good enough.
You run away from the adventure.
I am left behind with the broken inside me
    and memories that
are a struggle of life.
I can almost hear the reverberation when my
    heart becoming
more and more entangled with yours.
You will die for my vibe who have the strong
    root amidst
a fruitful tiny moment there you can feel my
    heartbeat.
Hesitating I try to break down every water
    pearl
and hope that they will be crushed and
    fly with
the wind into the horizon.
The broken inside me will embrace my mem-
    ories, make them fade,

and you will be left with my skeleton of an
    open fire
of inevitably bleed of scars you can`t heal.

OLD TRACKS

A witch or a guardian spirit
healing abilities appear as letters
on the wall
the gallows - sacrificial place by the
invincible paths of destiny
escaping - hidden from the hunting eyes
falling in love with one of the
dark heartless
love night's ordeal
hostage in the wilderness
tearful on the frozen ground
miserable chilled to the marrow
astray in the morning fog
the time of the beasts in the cold waves
from the ashes to the flames after
the storm
a scream in the dark in the frontier zone
the lonely battle of life and death
unwanted chaos back in old tracks...

COUNTRY GIRL

She kicked off her cowboy boots
picked up a cold beer
drink away her pain a little at a time
her scars was burning like a cigarette
in the midnight hour
still believe in the magic of the moon
occupied her soul
hopeless
fools like her never win
crushed the beer on the table
drop of bloods drip like her salty tears
deep shiver of desire and passion
until he turned into an untamed beast
a love undone in her broken heart
you wrapped her in chains and
barbed wire
within she is ashes from a dying rose
cursed and scattered in the darkness
from the devil's rainbow
disillusioned storm chases fragmented
hope....
-she is a fallen shadow of grief-

A GIRL'S DISASTROUS MELODY PATH

I wake up this morning
raises my weary head
where am I?
My skirt for a pillow
the earth is my bed
I have become the devil's temptation
on the run
I have no contact with the living
my mind speaks a language I don't
understand
my heart is waste -a ghost town-
my soul scare myself to death
I keep on running
I'm cursed and born in sin
whose daughter I am?
I have no conscience
I don't live for others or to
satisfy the world
I live to survive
I've seen too much death
and in my boots I have all I
need to protect myself
I don't know love, but I have feelings
for my horse I can't describe

-maybe it is love-
and don't dare touch my horse before
I lay five feet deep
because me and him are dances on
empty wallets
flashing back to a life I never had,
so I drown it out with leftovers
I find of old whiskey
who have I become?
I take my stallion back to the dusty
road of shades of tones of loneliness
this is my life
-grace of glory-

BRUSHSTROKE INTO ETERNITY

Her pretty smile hides the deepest story
-bleeding lips
Her eyes cries the most tears
-eyes of darkness
Her kindest heart has felt the most painful
-a heart of a soulless
She can't take it anymore
-do you know how much she misses you?
She can't get the melody of you out of
her head
-do you know how much she loves you?
...No you don't, but she does...
She is down on her knees.
Your shadow is haunting her
Your ghosts is chasing her
Your heart messing with her heart
Your lost soul looking for love in wrong bed
...and she wonders why...
Can you hear her demons screaming
at yours?
Can you hear her skeleton wants to play
with yours?
Can you hear her disaster are whispers
at your disorder?

...No you don't, but she does...
Her butterflies whistle after your obsession
because she wants to paint you as a
brushstroke into eternity.
It's time to color that white canvas with
your and hers heartbeats and vibrations
of shades of love
-lets make our hearts red again-

TIC-TAC, CAN`T FREEZE TIME

A little red house in the woods
perfect outside
Tic-Tac -Tic-Tac
the little girl grab her teddy bear
took her murky steps up the stair
Tic-Tac - Tic-Tac
she crawled into bed
squeezed the teddy bear
pierced her nose to it
can't freeze time
Tic-Tac - Tic-Tac
dark
scared
can't escape
can't sleep
Tic-Tac - Tic-Tac
footsteps
the big dark shadow appears from the
light in the hallway
Tic-Tac - Tic-Tac
he puts on his mask
she can't breathe
the smell is burning in her nose
her little tiny body knows what is

going to happen...
A big rough and cold hand takes off
her underwear
Tic-Tac - Tic-Tac
it hurts
silence tears
screaming within
can't fight against everyone's hero
Tic-Tac -Tic-Tac
sounds
wet…
naked…
cold…
blood…
pain…
shakes inside…
brave smile…
nauseous…
The little girl no longer hears the
clock from the living room
for this time he is done
she will never be done
a robbed body
inside the little red house in the woods
a little girl with big blue crystal eyes
sparkling of fear
squeezed the teddy bear
perfect outside
Tic-Tac - Tic-Tac....

THE BLACK BRIDE

At the Devil's workshop
she read his mind
don't play with it
and waste his time,
but she loves your play,
and he fools her in
her heart was screaming -stop-
he laughed and whispered
"You are my black bride
since you stabbed your man"...
That dark blood has remained
and twisted into her paint
her evilness dances on her ribs
a sadness twisted around her pain
insane she was on the surface
in silence she prayed to the angels of the
    red moon
and the sun of blood will soon arise
a lonesome sonnet gaze from her eyes
burned into her tattooed flowers of sadness
a face of death she's covering her dreams
    of you
touched her in places where the darkness
    used to appease

you put the lake from the Virgin forest on fire
a distant fog creeping inside her veins
she surrender into his destiny
of one tear of blood
a mysterious smile and an eagle's eye
he whispered "your hymen smell delight
and my horns is aroused"
a demon love painfully within
an altar of skull and one of her bone
she was searching for
suddenly she realized that he
had slaughtered her at that night when the
    Evil returned,
and she enrolled in the Devil's Pact in
the Black Book before she was born...

MY MIRROR ALLURES ME TO THE ASHES

I look in the mirror
time has burned scars in my skin
I still hunt for the missing parts of me
I still search for the beauty in me
I still reach for something I`m longing for
-I don't know what it is-
I have looked among the rocks
-but there was nothing-
I have been seeking thoroughly
between the stars
every star is shining bright
-doesn`t belong to me-
I have sifted the grain of sound in
my desert
even scavenge moving on
they only leave the cartilage behind
I'm still lost in the dark
walking around restlessly
like a miserable lonely ancient ruin
I'm still nobody
nobody lives with me
nobody crawls inside all over me
nobody is an echo in my silence
nobody is my tears

nobody is my powerful force to how
my soul falls apart
nobody is my fear deep within
and I look down most of the time
so you can't see my lost shine
and if you dare to turn on my button
to my sapphire moonlight and
embrace my crime
maybe my soul is home with a heart
that understand
until then I see myself getting fade
from the mirror
she is about to disappear
my mirror allures me to the ashes
she is nobody and useless is my middle
name and nothing is my surname...

FORBIDDEN ECHO

A dark autumn night the sky was falling
down with rain and the
pebbles were slippery
she had to go through the dark alley
her heart pounded hard with fear
she glimpsed him from the corner
of her eye
he was sitting on the bridge
it illuminated evil from his eyes
hunting
she held her breath and listened
heartbeat
abruptly she stood with her hands up the
wet wall
stars in her eyes and a cotton mind
she threw her head back, and he grabbed
her hair
his sharp claws pressed into her
milky-white skin
she felt his reptile tongue lick on her throat
slowly- tenderly - passionately
she could smell him
goose flesh
she glimpsed his rainbow-colored skin

spellbound
he was a secret between her shadow
and her soul
her whole body was in fiery blaze
he whispered her beauty with a
softness enchanted
her voice began to break
two predators love each other
their love is forbidden
the tears from their hearts turned
into a killing lust for sin
paralyzed from the blood moon of grief
they howled,
and they are the forbidden echo
of the love scenes.

THE GIRL IN THE GLASS BUBBLE

Her homeland was in a glass bubble
not a fairy tale bliss, but
a world of horror souls.
She scratched the glass bubble, but
it was she who stayed cracked
and shattered.
Everything she saw was her own reflection
- she hated it.
She was surrounded by happy kids, they
smiled, laughed and played together
something she didn't understand
what was.
They did not see her.
They did not hear her
- horrific curdling screams.
She was the weak link.
She stopped with what she loved most
-to draw.
With stifled tears she was sitting watching
the stars and for each shooting star she
wanted a graveyard.
In the glass bubble she is buried alive and
tormented to death.
She is like antique missing pieces inside

with demons that can't dance, but
they know the price of revenge.
She was always the lure girl for souls in
fake disguise.
Hiding her enclosed being is an
unresolved truth.
A truth others around her won't want
to come out.
Black sky and her demons are getting
worse than evil, and she become
dangerous when she learned to
control her feelings...

SUMMERTIME SADNESS

She got drunk
tried to drink away her pain
danced on the table
sang the saddest songs she knew
as elegant as the candle light
sparkling on the piano her Bambi eyes
was like sapphire moonlight
her hair flow like a river and her
cheery lips was telling magic
her radiance got the heartbeat of all
men in the bar to tremble,
but she had no longing to them...
The smell of whiskey and blue smoke
lay like a blanket over the room
remembering nothing until she
wakes up on a street corner with him
beside her
everything turned upside down inside her
you held her hair
you told her how beautiful she was
regardless
so much love for her
a day four years ago she turned her back
on him and said no, just go...

A choice she could sell her soul to the
devil for...
If she could turn back time...
You are still her best friend
doing everything for each other
having fun
conversation from dusk to down
know everything about each other
every time your name appears on
the phone her heart quiver in pain that
hurt so good
always a perfect picture of your family
suddenly, you knock on her door
she lets you in
she smiles bravely.
Her heart cracks
her eyes are bloodshot
you trace your fingertips down her jaw
she gasps for the breath
before their lips meet, time stand still
at this moment, and she can feel your
goosebumps on your nose
and your lips are drawn towards each other
she moans for both of you
drown in your emerald green eyes
just one last night in the sky of lovemaking
in sin he whispers
-I want to make love to you-
slowly they make love in
a body language only they knew
when tomorrow comes she has
pulled the trigger
she can't bear anymore
summertime sadness
they find her in the bubble bath with
rose petals from the
Black Rose...

RUNNING WITH THE WOLVES

In a covenant long ago she wrote in
blood where her life is written
down into eternity
if she dies she will come again and
lead the whole pact
her eyes look towards the forest
the moon rises and shines over her
she has one chance
it's time now
she run
she run with the wolves
she can watch and listen
feel
the sky is on fire
it is completely open
freedom
nothing can hurt her now
battered, but the scars grow
she`s running like a dancing elf
among the wolves she is safe
they look after her
they are hunting
kills
eats

sleeps
on the run
she runs with the wolves tonight
they have seen the dark side
behind the moon
her mind give her fear
she has blood on her lips
she's feels like home
stronger now
heartbeat
breath and her mind heals
stop hiding
she's all now
her spirit dances in the flame of
the ocean,
her crying shadow dances in the
moonlight and shines in the dark
the wolf's stops running
they come closer
looks at her with shiny blue eyes
licking her mouth
together with the souls of the wolves
she becomes one
she is being guided now
-faith-

REFLECTIONS

Off guard - a shout in the dark
unusual - hunted down
wounded - crumbling
heartbeat - gushing blood
licking herself on the lips
always been different
her past
the hunting
thirsty
hunger
sunrise behind the mountains
jumping down from her secret place
running
she is tearing apart
piece by piece goes up in smoke and the
dust is taken by the wind
at the river she watches herself in the water
long hair like the midnight sun's color play
green eyes that sparkle like emeralds
lips like a witch
tongue skilled in ink
a body like the white night turns
upside down
she shudders

inadequate
touch the shining water
despises herself
shadows that threaten the landscape
not safe
embraces herself with pain
a predator - she feels it like a sin
a destiny - in the darkness
it was more than she could take
as, another warrior falls.

WHEN YOU LOSE SOMEONE

Watching you go
- your hand in mine loses grip
- slipping away
it's like no other pain
I'm lost without you
I can't breathe
I need you
I miss you
your spirit waving at me
your soul is the brightest I have ever seen
I hope your ghost will hunt me
and wipe away my tears
- hollow
- deep painful grief
my crying shadow is trying to hide
I will never stop sobbing
the memories burn me down to the ravine
stairs to heaven.......wrong side of nirvana...
A rope led down into the dark eternity
I can't handle this anymore
I know I find you there...
You have an hourglass that you
received as a gift
there are the days that slowly

flow down,
and you can look back to the
Garden of Eden
where it began under the fig trees of life.
I'm sitting here alone, so puzzled
Because nobody knows so well what
that means to miss the one you love and
admire, maybe you must have experienced
this yourself to understand...
Because if tomorrow never comes...
-no one can cry all the tears for me-
I am lost -
did I in every way show him
how much
I love you.
Whatever the circumstances, always tell those
you love that you love them ...
Life is fragile.

MYSTERIOUS ROOMS

She's like a big house
with many rooms not found yet
no one wants to
no one is not brave enough
no one have a desire to dig into her
it's not lost
just hidden
lost control
on the edge
had been cut into pieces
can turn off the light
bad at love
like a ghost she haunts you
through walls and ceilings
she buries her soul within you
she wants a home
no one can give her
she is tired of being normal
will be invisible a bit
-because no one dares-
she is too mysterious..

LULLABY

Nobody knew how much she blamed
herself
she can't breathe in the end of the midnight
moonlight show her the path
she can't get him out of her mind
one picture bringing back so
many memories
she can't breathe in the end of the midnight
she can hear the angels voice
a silent Lullaby
he is her universe
she is just a little human on earth
dancing with the moonlight shadow
mesmerized
faithless
pain - tasted blood
shoot her, the voice of the death said
she believes - hell is all she catches
the devils Lullaby is awakening
nobody going to miss her
crawling on the floor
single bourbon on ice
a perfect storm in her head mixed with

a destroyed Lullaby on her jukebox
'cause this is where the country girl
slips away
she has bucked off.

A SUMMERNIGHT

Her Norwegian blood
red as the evening sun
runs in her Viking veins
which is as blue as the glacier
her skin is milky white
like the cold winter snow
she dances between mountains
and valleys where waterfalls
flow down to the fjord
a summer night with flowers
in the hair
a dress that flutter in the wind
she is like a fresh blossoming
of black roses with a touch
of red darkness
has lit a flame
has won a battle
it crackles in the joyful fire
with a mark of love
like the rainbow signs under
the clouds
as unique as every snowflake
she swims under the stars

in the moonlight of the night
in the ocean of romance.

MY BLACK STALLION

When no one can save her
invisible heroes
she takes her Black Stallion with a name
after the dark, shines blue in
the sun's rays
gallops into the sunset
freedom
maybe this time memories
fade into the ocean
dreams are so alive
day's like a slow train ticking by
all she can hear is your
words haunting her
can't get the melody out of her mind
she wonders if she is past the
point of rescue
often she hopes her life is a fairy tale
in a horror movie
she can't close the door to her heart
she swears she would never fall like this again.

SHADES OF BLACK SCARS

She tries to find peace because
her heart will heal
it's beautiful, but worn
it has been attempted repaired
with needle and thread
if you look closely, you can see
the shade of the stitches
torn off time after time
looking even further in,
deep behind her heart, you can watch
a glimpse of a face
it is like the shadows waving in the wind
you realize that the face belongs to the
heart, because they are equally ghostly
she turns her face away in disgust and
loathing
it storms in the heart's rhythm
faster and faster, she won't be anymore
it is like thorns from "the black rose" being
thrown at her, and she feels an
indescribable pain in her heart and it's
burn in her soul
In the face behind the heart tears flow like
a waterfall

As a veil, they embrace her heart and dig
"the river of tears" bigger and deeper
tears from a darkness that no little girl
should know about
tears from a scared soul that a soul never
should know about
tears from a place within a little girl never
knew she had a stolen body...
but always a soul and a
heart that she hid and protected
can she be whole again?
Is the last flame extinguished?
She can feel her heartbeat, breathes deeply
her body remembers
the heart knows
her mind can deceive her
all the emotions and experiences are
stuck in her body as the pain of a thorn
-Demons are screaming the worst
she can sense-
her eyes can't stop crying, her soul is
working to heal, her mind is trying to
connect with her heart
a thousand broken pieces of her heart is
laying beside her in a coffin of sorrows
with all her scars she begins to feel the
various nerves of the black paths
trails she never wants to join again
they'll be with her to the end of life, and
she'll try everything she can to make new
paths bright and beautiful next to the dark
ones...

PRINCE OF THE DARKNESS

She hears you shouts at night and
your voice is filled with grief.
Her curtain fluttering and
she can feel your breath.
She lifts her hand to her heart,
and it`s like drums, and she can't
stand still.
Her spirit dances in flames
along with demons and elves
in the night sky.
She follows you wherever you go.
She needs you and admires you,
take her with you.
She's yours.
She has nothing to be afraid of.
You're not dangerous.
The Dark prince comes closer with his
violent tongue.
You scream her name.
She continues to dance around in circles.
The wind grabs her soul
and you grab her heart.
Her spirit stops for a moment.
Need help from the goodness of light,

cherishes for her freedom,
but she can`t resist your beauty.
Your poisonous heart is like a snake
who wrapped around her,
and she can't breathe.
Please, put an end to her pain.
You laugh and throw off your shadow.
In the flames you grow large and powerful.
She's lost.
She's yours
Spirit and soul,
believe and fight
live and die.

UNWRITTEN DESTINY

Inferno in her heart
her sacred black rose of
darkness are being colder
inhaling the scent of her essence
under the moon of shaken sadness
she is dancing with her archangel
our bodies getting drenched in
Angels tears from heaven
make her scream your name
in vain across your black eyes
penetrate her soul
her pain are the echoes of
dust you can hear rattle within
with a wolf heart she has
been thrown out to the pack
fighting for life unwritten destiny
in her chapter of love
the unspoken voice in the soulless wind
changing her shadow
her spirit of the darkened path
perhaps she will return leading the pack...

YOU BORROWED HER HEART

You caught her heart and
lent it for a while
you embraced her with
all your love and caring
she was lost in your soul
at one point you gave her
the heart back
a broken heart with pain
she became a dark crushed soul
emptiness within
it's far too much to take
she almost drowning in her
own tears of ocean
now she has dried out
an Angels tears of blood
falls down her cheek
with her bloody eyes
she digs her grave of sorrow
and hope death will knock with
his skeleton on her coffin.

CAGE OF DEFEAT

She is chained with barbed wire
in a cage and it will be the
death of her
in an endless emptiness
is an old friend
the sweet grief
she is a mess and her misery
have no end
she is not bulletproof
bending like a broken rose
with thorns stretching up the
sky full of stars
she climbs up to experience endless
heavenly view
a magical mystery ride on her
favorite star
when the world is beating her down
in the cage of defeat.

MIDSUMMER NIGHT

In the sunset on a beach in the world
somewhere a girl dances around the
bonfire to the music in her mind
she danced like nobody was watching
she danced of the rhythm of her heartbeat
her spirit in the sky
elves in the flames
nymphs in the ocean
lures and plays
from the forest shadows the trolls are
blinked with their eyes
a Hulder is waving her tail and
licking around the mouth with her
poisonous tongue
a wonderful delight night
scary night
among sorcery and magic
that girl danced herself into
the heart of the key to the
Midsummer night treasure.

ANGEL OF DEATH

She is laying in a bed of dreams
of nightmares
like a wave on the ocean her
hair rests on the pillow
she looks like an angel
someone said
maybe the angel of death
she can hear her soul whisper
your name
she has lost her way
hollow inside
salty drops falling from her
eyes of honesty
memories of you cover her heart
constant pain
will it ever stop hurting
every thought is shadowed by you
she grabs a needle and thread
tries to sew her scars
she will never feel hurt again.

EMOTIONS

A feeling
embraces my
heart and soul
where my spirit
hunts around
in eternity for
answers
then I realize
...I wanting what
does not exist...

WRECKED SOUL

She feels like a ghost inside
yet sparkling eyes shining
as the rays of the midnight sun
that descend behind the mountain
she cries drops of glass that are crushed in
the ocean somewhere
where the waves roll up towards the beach
she looks at the horizon where clouds turn
into stars
an indescribable longing for an
indescribable memory for
an indescribable heartbeat
like a black rose that will never unfold
their rose petals
as a swan she bends her head in relentless
heartache
you don't dare to touch her wrecked soul.

SHADES OF LOVE

She wants you to feel the presence
of her soul in your bare body
through every word she writes
she wants you to feel that she spread
several shades of love onto you
let your life flow over her
cover this walls of fear with passion
make love to these labyrinths of darkness
discover every inch in this broken heart
reveals every touch of her ink in her
mind with your burning flames of love
embrace her within
in the end she has to close her diary
you are only in her mind
but still so alive.

AROUSED

She is a fantasy in your mind
but is alive.
She watches your spirit dance over the sky
as the stars in her eyes.
She feels your heartbeat as
the waves in the ocean.
She wants to take her wings and fly
but the moon is in between.
She feels like a ghost.
He can't touch.
She`s using her intuition.
He use his imagination.
She is a treasure.
He will never will find equal.

YOU AND ME

You and me together
the road is long
we are together
is possible
you watch me
the night is long
we kiss
you and I dance
in the name of love
looking up to the moon
aiming at it
and if we miss
we end up among the stars
you and I can't hide that
we are enthralled
between our pages
in the book
of the longing.

THE SKY IS CRYING

If I only knew
the days were slipping past
good things never last
heaven is crying into my face
I change this drops into tears
I feel like I am done
the darkness has won
I am lost
it can tear my soul apart
in my heart you have remained
I take my fragile wings and fly away
I can`t hide
I can`t run
let get lost together
in the pain
until the light comes pouring
through my eyes you and I can
dance in flames of the darkness.

COLORLESS

She takes her final steps.
Here she calls her home.
She turns around and sees her own footsteps.
She didn't realize they looked like this.
She feels that one foot stands out from the
    other.
It's like her footsteps trying to tell her
    something.
Her footsteps are everywhere in this place.
So much emotion.
She just wants to wipe them away.
She will soon be on a journey.
A journey where she will color all colors in
    the rainbow,
in the wind and in her colorless wings.
She envisions a white butterfly.
Feeling through heavy headwinds.
Fall.
Lives lifeless on the ground.
She strokes it gently.
She sees a small wound in the fragile body.
It will always be a scar.
She lifts it up to the sky.
Hope it is strong enough to fly.

The butterfly's feelings move up and down.
Turns its wings slightly.
Raises up and flies.
Long away from the horizon it is just a black
    shadow.
In her hand, the butterfly's imprint is again.
Dust shines like glitter in her hand,
in all possible colors.
So the white colorless butterfly was not quite
    white anyway ...
It just hid its beauty.
Maybe someday everyone sees how
beautiful the colorless and white butterfly is ...

PANTHER

Last night you were a panther.
One of the most beautiful animals in the
But, also one of the most dangerous.
Listed around in the nature of darkness
With glittering coat and shining eyes.
You hunted.
Circle your prey.
You can feel the silence.
You stretched out your paw,
washed it gently,
before planting it in the wet surface.
You smelled in the night.
Licked your mouth
and jumped up to the nearest tree.
At the top you looked over the landscape.
Felt hunger, starvation and desire.
You have to kill tonight to survive.
You closed your eyes, a panther was your
    destiny
in this life.
You were attacked, smashed kisses and the
    heart torn out.
No magic.
No beautiful words.

No one cares.
No one miss you, just coldness and darkness.
Quietly you go from the place.
This time satisfied.
You won this fight.
You sneak home.
Lie down.
Lick your wounds.
You know it's not long to the
next hunger
next yearning
next desire
the next battle.
Die or survive.

WITHOUT ME

It was days and I loved life.
Suddenly everything was turned upside
    down.
I got scared.
I thought the worst, and I
Can't stop it.
It is from the past that puts their blanket
over me and I choke.
I can't breathe, but I know
I love you.
Without me, I think you have to go
further without me.
I don't deserve you.
You deserve so much better than me.
I can't stop this now.
I have opened my heart for you and that
    hurts.
I love you.
You love me.
We love each other.
I never believed in love.
Maybe my inner soul was already trying to
Tell me something then.
You are perfect even time goes by.

You always make me smile, but now
tears are easier to catch.
I smile bravely, but I have to
Do this without you.
You make me feel good, though
You have to move on now.
You deserve so much better than me.
I don't deserve you.
I will not stand in the way of your happiness.
I can't make you whole and good anymore.
I'm scared and it hurts.
A pain I don't want to feel but I have to.
I can't let you follow me, you
Don't understand it yourself.
You have to take care of you.
I don't know my future.

I just know my past now.
Without me, I think you have to go
further without me.
I don't deserve you.
You deserve so much better than me.
I can't stop this now.
Can I catch you if you fall?
I can't do, I am broken.
You have to find a new safe port now.
I have to move on from here, though
I don't know where.
It may not be the way to go
which is the brightest and where the sun
    shines.
Maybe I have to go into a darkness
that I don't Know, again.
I'm afraid. I lost my grip.
I love you so it hurts.
I can't take you further into my inner soul
and heart.

You have to save yourself.
I don't know if I'm going back.
Time will show..
I know I can't demand that you wait for me.
I ask you to go, I go.
Our roads separate here.
Maybe my heart tried to tell me something.
I chose not to listen, but it has been
Completely fantastic.
Now I have to find the magic in my life again.
I can't let you join in there.
You deserve better than me.
I'm afraid.
I am not brave.
I love you.

TRUST

She will never trust you.
It's not your fault.
She can trust people outside her
comfort zone.
She doesn`t master having faith in
someone in close relationships.
She has been overused and wounded.
It's hurt so bad, incredibly painful.
Show her your grace.
Maybe a butterfly should not be in cages.
A butterfly will fly wherever it wants.
She doesn`t want to be if you are thinking
about leaving.
She will not be cheated with.
She does not want to be lied to.
She can't trust you.
You are the most beautiful person she knows.
It hurts so bad.
To feel the grief in her heart over
something she has.
She has something valuable that no one
    else has.
You help her keep her head above the water.
When the day comes, she can't love you.

At night her are just yours.
Then she feels alive.
For every breath it stings all over her.
She can't find peace.
She hopes she does not lose your imprints
that you leave behind.
She need you by her side.
But she can't trust you.
She just can't make it.
Everything is hurting and it is not your fault.
She can't feel your heartbeat.
You always take her breath away.
She is broken.
There is nothing you can do.
Their flame didn't last forever anyway.
It's like her fading.
But she can't live without you either.
She dies inside when she thinks of you.
She tries to get you out of her mind.
Ever little part of her is solved with
ever little peace of you.
Heartbreaking, each side up and down.
All the scars you leave in her heart.
Inside, she blooms like a ghost.
You break her heart and she has no answer.
Tears are her words that her mouth can't tell.
People never forget how you made them feel.
It's not your fault.
That girl is a mess.

SOULS OF LOVE

He put his strong arms around her,
and she melted in his arms.
She felt his love and energy burn
around in her body.
She felt safe as he surrounded her in
nature's own wilderness.
Only the two alone against the dangers
of darkness.
Only the two alone against the longing
for love.
Only the two alone against forbidden love.
His eyes told her about sorrow and pain.
Her eyes told him about unknown waters.
He makes her do things she thought she
should never do.
She becomes a slave to his lovemaking.
They cannot remove each other's heartbeat.
They throw away each other's time.
Hope they will be happy in others
arms one day.
They spend a lot of time on a battle that
is already lost.
They tear each other's world apart.

Their hearts bleed and their souls have
caught each other.
They have given each other's life to eternity.

THE BLUE BEAUTIFUL EYES

She could feel every touch and give him the
whole sky full of stars.
She melted in his glance and colored more
of her wings.
She will always love him and now she can
not live without him.
She disappeared in his eyes and the world
stood still.
She misses him every second and feels her
body's longing.
He takes her fragile wings and spreads out
in the dark of night.
He puts his strong arms around her with
all his love.
He looks at her with his blue eyes, they
glitter like diamonds.
His blue eyes look deep inside her broken
heart.
He looks far into her soul.
She's caught.

BATTLE CRY

She lit up a cigarette after turning the tables
around in the saloon
drinking too much
that country girl never said no to a fight
after 3 rounds of billiards.
A battle cry.
You gave her bruises, but she ended up
    singing
your song all the way home after she was that
girl crawling on the floor.
She is a mystery you have a desire to
    solve and
you have to explore her like a treasure map.
She became one of your portraits in your
    diary.
She tried so hard and get so far, but you are a
memory of a time when she fell apart.
Your voice painted hope in her mind, and her
head you filled up with a bouquet of red
    roses.
Her soul you filled up with deep affections
deeper than the universe
and you decorated her with
sequins that sparkled in the twinkle from

your eyes.
She still rhymes after your might and the
full force of liar, but she is about to design
her own rhyme.
She wash her heart clean from your poison
and our twisted fate by drinking holy water.
She putted her trust in you, now she has
     to pick
up her own pieces from her battle with you.
Your hypocrisy.
It hurts.
Watch you go.
She closed the door.
Catch her breath.
Scream.
Tried to kill you with her spell.
The Queen was crowned, but it was not her.
She thought she was your star, but in her
darkness she was invisible and her fear
evolving and is a reality.
That girl had to fall to lose it all
no one can save her now
is this her slowly goodbye
is it worth fighting for herself in this
     battle cry…

A BEAUTIFUL OLD BASSLINE

She, a country girl takes her old guitar
and glues the strings back together
an old bassline grows in her mind
she can't repair her broken heart or her
dead soul and her ghost can't move her
mood along
you are her melody, chemistry and
memory
a beautiful pain
not a thorn less rose,
but he who dares not to grab the thorn on
the Black rose should never claim
to love her
a heavenly escape in hers words of a
melody where the moon sleeps to her
humming
he wrote a stunning story over her scars
she painted him in charming new shades
of colors from hers merciless salvation
she lost her heart into him,
and she put her soul into his flame
of passion of love between two spirits
she was burned
all my music notes to calm the ashes was

taken by the wind wave
she destroyed herself the most
you never convicted for a felony
a pleasing cheater in her bed
she`s tearing your picture apart
she was ready to die
she decided you wasn't worth it
now I'm the outsider that slithers slowly
inside you and when you feel suffocated
it is only me who knocks on your throat
and black worms you`re yellowing vomiting,
because she wants you to feel a taste
of delicious old me...

SAVAGE LOVE

Hunting me
Catch me
Enjoy me
Love me
Dance with Me
Turn me on
Release out your flame
I am untamed and wild
In you, I am tears
Break into me
Whisper the tears from my heart
Whisper the shadow of my soul
Let the night and your ecstasy
come and my wings of art
follow your shapes of your body
like a piece of jewelry
I growl lightly and my red lips form
the secret unspoken words
Like a common swift you embrace your
arms around me
I am like a white wind
I climb down the red path where
the blood rushes
Hips and mountains move like

the waves of the ocean
I open up
A rose bursts into full bloom
The rain is falling
You play with my hair
and you lift me up
and out playing the whole orchestra ....
- and our symphony of savage love will
play again and again on everyone's heart
strings and the echo never ends...

SIN OF A RUIN HUMAN

I look at you and I`m home.
But, I don`t use my eyes
I see you with my heart
I listen to you with my soul
I touch you with my heartstrings
and I embrace your hell and
transforms it and makes it look like
a work of art
and our blood makes history
in our fairy tale bones when my
skeleton rattled up your
naked skin to knock
on yours sin of a ruin human disguise
by a demon of darkness
kissing my mind, and we
enjoyed the pain
when we were screaming in
heroin hurricanes from
eternal sadness of a masterpiece.

THE SHADOW DANCE

Her smiling shadow dance among
the death
her grief are laying breathless
under the devil`s bones
the virgin from the forest of the fog
whisper her silently prayers
evoking her madness
her venomous heart is rhyming to the
lost zombie`s rattled skeletons
her wicked mind whistles of a
melody darker than the
-Prince of darkness-
an evil light from red eyes are follow every
step she makes
only Hell can touch her milky white skin
only her demons are playing
on her memories of painful tears
she is the ashes from barbarian love
from torture
her silhouette is like a dying rose
her faith is signed in blood
a vision softly creeping
-not to be reborn-

MY CRYSTAL SHADOW

All my black rose petal bleed inside
infinity darkness
a resurrection is aroused
and now my beauty in each petal
are like dark red heartstrings
maybe an angel in disguise
only one MAN try to dare
he fell in love with my diamond tears
he pierced my silver scar and echoes fears
and my crystal shadow he
fills up with glittering pieces of love
and my shimmering crystal bathed in
our beyond midnight battles
mystical universe creations of moments
powered by broken dreams
our souls remnants of war
slowly put piece by piece
of me together
but you`re still searching in my labyrinths
to find the key to my eternal glue
for my cracks in my heart
in unknown melodies
and rebellious rhyme

you enchanted
me with your spell of secrets.

SOUL TO SOUL

When my soul meets another soul and
    my soul
Recognize a piece of myself deep within the
other, and we both feel it,
And if your soul tickling my mysterious
    chamber
in my heart,
and if your ghoulish soul howl to the
    moon and
buried secrets kept within crypts un-
    derground,
and you have a bizarre imagination beyond
harrowing nightmares,
and if you have a feeling of being torn
    apart from
monsters inside you,
and they are knocking on your bones,
and your tragic memories are crawled around
    your mind
-our souls are completely spellbound-
Is a soul connection
In our dungeon where darkness plays and
You and I

Are a masterpiece of the painful burning
    inferno…
If not, my spirit will hunt yours…

FROZEN TEARS FROM A WINTER MOON`S SORROW

In the wilderness night she is trying to
create her own snow angel with hope
gazing up to the blue moon
the shadow of the moon has scars that
     sparkle
red colors.
Snowflakes descend on her nose that
burns like her tears
when they hit the ground they crush like
     crystal
her grief is bottomless and unresolved
her sadness is the gateway to redemption
frozen tears from a winter moon`s sorrow
to know her sadness in silence she is
searching for something she can`t reach
she is off the deep end
like the moon she is embraced with a red
color, but it is not sparkling
she didn`t notice she cut herself with a
frozen teardrop, sharp as a knife
maybe a sign from above
will she awaken the phoenix or the demons
in your soul
in the embers of broken hearts her life

is a shadow of ghosts in dark rising,
and she will never shine anywhere else
even the moon`s sorrow is jealous because
the moon never can bury himself in a coffin
she whispers your name and frosty smoke
    spelled out
"death is not ready yet to haunt you"
frozen tears from a winter moon`s sorrow
remains a mystery
you are the silhouette of her heart in
every painful moments
until their hearts touch
she is just a vibe you can`t find nowhere else.

WHEN THE SKY IS CRYING BLOOD

When the sky is crying blood
I have lost my Luna
I`m in the lions cave
my secret friend
our treasure of a place
paradise
alone and in danger with my illusion
the ocean bring your waves and the thunder
a glowing light near the surface
under the blackened sky
make me believe in
-once upon a time-
a touch and a firestorm ignite the river
between our twisted souls
I`m terrified
a world on fire
sadness burning in our hearts
with my lions eyes I will watch over your
freedom
when the sky is crying blood
I will rise.

A WOLF HEART CHANGING SHADOW

Inferno in her heart
Her sacred black rose of darkness
are being colder
inhaling the scent of her essence under
the moon of shaken sadness
she is dancing with her archangel
tears from heaven make her scream
your name in vain across your black
eyes penetrate her soul
her pain are the echoes of dust
you can hear rattle within
with a wolf heart she has been thrown
out to the pack
fighting for life
unwritten destiny in her
chapter of love
the unspoken voice in the soulless wind
changing her shadow
her spirit of the darkened path
perhaps she will return leading the pack…

LIKE THE OCEAN

Her emotions are like the waves on the ocean
up and down
in and out
because to you, she was the entire ocean
a little gem on the bottom
a little treasure at the beach
a little word as a grain of sand in the
deep secret of the ocean
she is sparkling like the magic of
the rainbow
then you drowned her and broke her
heart badly
and spread her pieces from her heart
and soul into the horizon
like a seed with the wind and when
the ocean is in peace
deadly calm
deep beneath lies her fate and rest
she can`t forget
follow no rules
picks up the pieces of her heart
feels like broken glass in her mouth
like the ocean

no one can tame her
she whispers words of resurrection.

MY MISCHIEVOUS EYE
SPARK

I`m not an innocent girl, to deal with
me you have to be brave, deal with
your own darkness and the "devil`s back"
because this girl has a darkness of secrets
-no one has dared tried to deal with
but my demons are what drove him wild
together with
my dangerous
my tragedy
my madness
my pain
my sin
and all my monsters of nightmarish
origins from the moon beam
I want to give him heaven
I`m not the devil`s daughter,
but he wanted my HELL
and my mischievous eyes spark
that what made him love me-

CAN I BE HER

I don`t want to think
I don`t want to remember
I don`t want to sit under a
tree and tremble
I don`t want to be on this
melancholy place
I don`t want to be lost in my chains
I don`t want to be a prisoner in my
own life

I just want to love
I just want to be with you in the spotlight
I just want to be that girl you talk about
in your stories
I just want to be that girl you sing every
word about
I just want to be that girl you say
the words to:
I love you

I just want to be in your arms and
let you embrace me with all of you
I just want to be that girl you wipe

tears on
I just want to be that girl you pull
out from the wrecked skeletons
and be safe.
Can I be her?

PUT HER MIND TO REST

A tongue twisted like the devil`s wings
a love of coat of armour
I can`t purify my heart from the poisoning
I can feel the excitement as my
thoughts begin to bleed
a cold night
reminds flashbacks
demons cry in my mind
hunted by souls in the dark
my bones shivering
you write on her blank sheets
working hard and saving
help her to put her mind to rest.

THE GIRL IN THE BROKEN MIRROR

She looks in the mirror
she is lost, cold and sad
she crushes the mirror
blood flows from her hand
it hurts, but not as bad as her
pain within
she is scared, alone and miserable
she picks pieces by herself
up bite for bite
again after being shattered
she didn`t want to live
she didn`t want to die
she knows that death gives no return
She wants to disappear.

A VISION OF THE NIGHT'S SUN MIRACLE

Far in the woods she lives in a country far
    from everything
known for its adventures of trolls, barn gob-
    lins and elves
among wild animals, where earth and
    sky meet
the north wind grabs her long, bright hair
a small sign of life in the forest
she`s been call Huldra, but no light pillar of
    angels
with her sweet red candy lips, she plays
    the harp
with mood and charm she dances into the
    northern lights
that glow in the night sky
tonight's sun miracle becomes a vision of
    sunrise
her curse is an extended promise
a raven among her imagination speaks of a
    night's dreamer
where rivers of blood gushing, and she is
    on fire
glorious sound of her high notes from a
    magical

song from her primordial stream flowing in
      her veins
her legacy can never change
a black heart
the dark side of the moon gives her a spark
she speaks the words that catches the eye
      among the trees
to ignite a red color
burning red satisfaction
she hears the devil playing his violin
together they create a vicious circle of a cruel
      night
with a liquid from a virgin they believe in
      eternal beauty
her ghostly grace suffocates her sordid past,
      but the smoke
is reviled in every breath
in addition, her invaders desecrated the
      temple
slayed her soul, and she became an untamed
      beast of a beauty
of the fiercest storms.

AGAIN?

I burned my tongue with a flame from my
        bonfire only because
to taste your ashes from your soul
I blew smoke rings and waved goodbye under
        a weeping moon
it soaks my breath out of my lungs, must have
        one whiskey bottle
to my mouth, I going to run this Halloween
        party and play
with myself
you was my everything, but you were looking
        for love
in wrong bed....again....
A loser like me never win
I`m done haunting you....again...
I`m done with you...again...
I swore I`d never fall like this...again?....
My dark memory, black sheep, sad chapter
A roadside bar in the countryside
everyone thinks she is crazy
I don`t mind
has always been misunderstood
has always met turnpike on my path
living on the edge

waiting for the skid row
taking myself to the end of the line...again...
Never found, always invisible to the
     good guys
singing on her last blues
no more happy times
crushed dreams
an empty shell of a body
only black, cold and darker than the
     graveyard
cases of a broken soul
only zombies and scavengers are fighting in-
     side her
sucking marrow, tendons and ligaments
an eternal itching and spitting blood
my rotten flesh and rattle bones are crawling
     back
to the chains...again...
Again? don`t touch me, you won`t open the
     door to my
dark paradise, because,
I will again burn my tongue
only to taste you....

RED MOONBEAMS

My mind still keeps reminding how much it
misses your hands braided in my hands
your legs embraced my legs and your
words lurking out my sparkle in my
eyes and the devil in my smile
when you hear my snickering laugh and
you watch my lips reaches the celestial
peak of bliss when we were together
you developed a deep thirst in me,
and you`re yearning awestruck after my
Angels black rose sigh
you felt my tightened passionate squeeze
you pulled me in
I caught a sight of your
rude eternal satisfaction
beneath aroused shameful pain
vibration in my pounding heart
my shadow dancing around the
red moonbeams chasing our spirit
to a gleamed starved love scene
behind the trees with the man who
can't be moved by script
we could be bound together through
the same pain

I love you
you couldn't handle it
-and you run
I miss you...
tonight my ghost soul haunting
your shivering cold soul
and I will peel you alive with my
suction that suffocates you...

THAT GIRL

That girl show her burned and
massacred wounds
she yearns for souls with depths
deeper than world ocean`s
blue and dark souls who have
seen the furies in perdition
that girl rip off chains of this
mental cage however beaten
always a soul of the miserable
intertwined with the lost ones
a desire to fight
heart beating
soul singing
spirit rising
phoenix within catches her legacy
finally find home
solicitations to be your graveyard
please, bury her skeleton with conscience
after your demons have eaten her soul out
and you raise that girl spirit
to yours dark heart
of a dead soul in a permanent pain.

THE DANCE FLOOR OF
HEAVEN IN HELL

I felt a cold and bony hand in mine
two red dangerous eyes sparkled at me in a
moment of silence
a tongue whistling between your teeth
I listened to your wheezing
I felt your pulse increase
the demon dance created with devilish
    dreams
you have no shadow to hide
you touched me crystal shadow gently with
your claws
and your hands of sorrows
are the best tenderness I ever felt
your fate is sealed in a path that shall never
end before blood red tears scattered in
to the end of the galaxy
I know you are a destroyed soul
embraced your heart in armor
I faced my fear
your closeness makes my heart stop
you laid down your head on my
shoulder
cheek against cheek
heartbeats

raw emotions in every step you danced over
the dance floor of heaven in hell
a delicacy for my senses
you caught me in your worst nightmare
of the darkest treasure
a ghost scream inside me
untouched lips from being kissed
are feeding me with trembled words like
    nectar
hear our hearts loves chaotic in a melody of
sadness before they wither away
the way you`re holding me in your arms
    with a
slow seduction that starting a storm inside me
traced my desire to crave my hunger to
something I should be afraid of
then you took your clothes off and on your
chest written in blood I could read:
I want you and I will enjoy you, no return,
because I going to rip you
apart and die away...

THE LAKE OF FIRE AND BRIMSTONE

Your words tracing down my skin
they are like tattooed into my bones and it
    burns
my own mind dripping down like tears
my bleeding brain that you crave
is lingering in my thoughts
between your teeth you spell words
that create memories
with my bleeding ears
I listen to your enchanting words like a
    sorcerer
You`re drooling out
and hoping for magic
my tongue lick your face off
and your words going up in smoke
my shadow dancing in the fog
painting me a sign
SOS
My candy cotton lips sucking yours
a delicate delay of smirk
changes to a scream in nightmares
you never get rid of
do you want to belong in another story
do you turn on to mentally torment her

you rip of my wings
I was caught
always your girl on a pedestal
I will never touch our memories
must they burn in eternal damnation
in the lake of fire and brimstone
when can I breathe again without pain?

THE HEART OF YOUR PLAYGROUND

Yesterday autumn breeze whispered in my
ear : I can feel two broken hearts, but it is his
soul that trace over your soul every day...
My broken heart bleeds...and when it
      rained in
my heart you kissed every drop and
transformed them into memories
I've forgotten who I am
you took control over me
and my delicate ice crystals are transformed
into diamond dust and I will never breathe
because of the fear of losing you
and I can feel you choking my fractured
existence
when you suck my soul out of my pores
and it is playback through my skin it's slowly
crawls all over my body
I hope we never lose touch,
this is our playground and put me in your
canyon and let your natural hunger take care
of me in your kingdom
I feel your vibrations in your voice
touches my heart gently
you are macho but singing me love songs and

let our hearts speak
I can feel our chemistry as magnetism
      and you
can feel the invisible fire and when my tongue
came into play you`re gasping for more...
your science in theory you practice on
      me and
you gave me wings
to explore you...
Let me be your archaeological unsolved
mysterious phenomenon like the
extraterrestrial beauty she is in the shadow
of a drama of violent hearts that unfold
words are too painful to be spoken,
      cause your
eyes told me everything
I'm tired, no miraculous return
don't ever stop plying lyrics on my heart-
      strings
when winter throws a white veil and the color
palettes in our elements disappear, let us
shine acrobatically before a death sentence
      for
delicate souls...

I WAN THE WAR

My frozen tears play
a melody far inside
deep within my heart
it hurts like hell

I try to catch one
of my tears
sharp as a knife
hoping to cut
emotions out
that are hidden
in my bones

I sense blood
I believe I`m longing to
fall apart
I have a desire of
destruction
I stared into my
darkness of scars
I reach for all my
silently fragments
of my soul

at that moment I realized
I wan the war
not the peace…

THE BLACK ANGEL OF THE CEMETERY

She kneels in the cemetery
picking up pieces of her own skeleton
unsure if it is the wind that stroking her cheek
the bats fly in circles around her
screaming about the black angel of the
        cemetery
chasing her myth about her dark heartbeat
and whispering shadow
the raven sleeps
the owl is on duty on the upper branch
the moon is hidden behind a cloud
she lights candles
they form a ring of love and desire
a small light alone loses its darkness
together they are the flickering flames of
        flames
of the night's mood
cemetery - peace and harmony
grief and despair
life and eternity are united beyond
her ghost feel
the grief of eternity floods
through her heart
security and hope

she feels the good vibes in hiding
but do not dare to resurrect the violence of
    dreams
she looks at the candles
a little glow of the faith of the future
but tonight she is a chain
between life and death
carved one last greeting in stone
a drop of ink from her soul got people
to think
once a little girl who believed in dreams
she as an adult has long since lost
the silent thoughts
the snow falling
lays down like a bride in white over
unread graves
with real emotions of the words written
she has a skeleton's lovely construction of
beauty lines similar to the white lilies on her
    grave.

BLACK ICE BRIDGE OVER
RAINBOW WATER

She is defeated and broken
living with a tear in her eyes
darkness and scars all around her
looking for black ice bridge over rainbow
    water
a silver bullet will ease her pain
beaten and damned
rise and fall
-no more-
all the bodies lying in her hometown
dead to her
slayed them with her tongue that was cut off
defiant tone on her path
her weary widower marches
trying to hunt her
tired to fighting for people who was ok with
    losing her
she`s trying to save the pieces she can`t reach
her love was in caged and conceal the
battle lines wild violation
closer to the black ice bridge over rainbow
    water
she searches for the incinerate
let the fires just bath her

in her war of the many shades of color
let her world goes black
no more wicked spellbound romance
it was a heat wave sin
embraced with petal flares from a legendary
    rose with
a name from the darkest night
bursting with nightmares of nostalgic de-
    struction
like a loaded gun on a roller coaster fireball
and her misery of dark dreams
she`s captivating everyone with her spider
    dance
an angel become the devil
twilight is heaven to the lonely
standing at the edge of the black ice bridge
    over rainbow water
the black rose will find its home
she burns and goes up in flames and there`s
    always a page in
her book that hasn`t been read
she died to get in again…

THE GIRL IN THE BASEMENT

It's dark, cold and it smells bad
her eyes have grown accustomed to the dark-
    ness in which she stares lifelessly into
in her arm hook she holds on to her
    teddy bear
there is a clown of porcelain in the corner
    that follows her with
eyes on every movement she makes
next to the clown is a doll she has been trying
    to rip her eyes off
paralyzed with fear she knows what's coming
punch-kick-lugging-words
she sits in the corner of her mattress lying on
    the floor
hungry and thirsty
she finds insects and worms that she eats
whether it is day or night she does not know,
but she knows the night
they always come… and her heart and soul
    leave her physical body
she lies lifeless, but she cannot hide the fear in
    her eyes
they tie a ribbon around her head, and she is
    forced to close her eyes

but no one can change the blood band
she obeys, has stopped fighting then she does
     not have to be chained to the wall with
     barbed wire and scratched with a knife,
the scars remain around her wrists and ankles
she vomits, and she has to eat her own vomit
     for supper that night
she washes her panties in her own saliva, but
     it never gets clean
she listened for sounds…
Bottles rattling, furniture being thrown
     around, loud voices, a dog beeping, she is
     rocking back and forth
she cries hysterically and screams, she's scared
then she must take her punishment, she is
     disobedient
she spits blood and teeth fall out of her
     mouth
every bone in her body hurts
she can feel her face, but it's different,
     broken jaw
swollen eyes that she soothes with urine, and
     she lacks hair on one side
she hears later that they framed her hair and
     hung it on the wall
in kitchen with the words "her first haircut"
a black heart and a broken soul
anger, guilt, shame, panic, fear, these emo-
     tions is repeated all the time
she sits in the corner of her mattress in the
     basement…
everyone thinks this is a fairy tale, nobody
     knows this was her life ...

TEARS FROM THE WOLF`S EYES

My world burned to ashes and my days are
   darker
you turned on your charm, I`m just wanting
   to heal
this morning has broken and
my mind collides with every failed attempt to
comfort my own heartbeats
counting rocks on the bottom of my soul
   through
narrow never ending hallways
I'm knocked back inside my old track
it brings tears from the wolf's eyes
when you thought I was a princess from the
   fairy tales
I was the most wanted girl in town writing on
   a new chapter in my book
I am one big wave, you can't handle
I am the wings of the wind, you can't catch
I am the great mystery, you can't solve
I am a lonely wolf
a gentle harp is playing to my fragile heart
   and blue river soul
it brings tears from the wolf's eyes

a kissing flame from a lonely eagle flying
    above me,
and we fly wild together
the sky's symphony of spirits dancing in
    northern lights
and shadows from the wolves blow my
    emerald kiss to the
lost moon dreaming in the darkness,
and I am one of the heirs of the night
when the earth's breath meets the sunrise in
    the ocean
behind the songs of the wolves in the
    dreams of
ancient voices from white buffalo in the world
    of circles of life
and legends rhythm from the woods trumps
    my sweet lullaby
and I listen to the echoes from a friend
the voice of the death
there is an angel hanging from a tree in the
    forest.

UNDER THE NORTH STAR

The moon reflected the North star in your
    eyes,
tears rolled down like words that were hard to
    speak.
Our love is lost and a lifelong fire is dead.
My brain went in error.
I know I never had wings and my witchery is
    clearly toxic.
I know I have to play for my wickedness and
    pain,
but I can`t sacrifice the dark side of the
    thinking moon and
be fearful of the night.
I cried out your name under the North star
holding on to your pocket.
I tried to swallow you through my unicorn
    lips in silence.
We always drank Jack Daniels after we make
    love and
you always had to blow a cool breeze and
    soothe my damp
skin under the North star.
You always had me with words lovingly
    whispered

through actions unspoken.
Now I have to unbolt you.
Your blood has stopped flowing.
You changed direction without me.
Now I have to see the way you shine
    without me.
I can`t escape from the dead echoes haunt
    from behind,
words grasping at my mind.
You did my grave when you kissed my bones,
    shared lies and secrets,
but I didn`t understand.
I killed the illusion of you.
Now I am a falling star trying to fit in to the
unknown darkness under the North star.

ABOUT THE AUTHOR

To learn more about Orkidedatter and discover more Next Chapter authors, visit our website at www. nextchapter.pub.

Beautiful & Battered
ISBN: 978-4-82412-056-4
Mass Market

Published by
Next Chapter
1-60-20 Minami-Otsuka
170-0005 Toshima-Ku, Tokyo
+818035793528

6th December 2021